This is the Book I Wrote

By Pat Goldys

Thanks To-

Kathy Vicarini, my sister, who created the graphic organizers for the aspiring writers.

Shauna Bidgood, the amazing librarian at Mars Estates Elementary in Baltimore County. Shauna provided student samples from her class writing lessons.

Elizabeth McLaughlin's grade 3 students at Mars Estates Elementary in Baltimore County. Her wonderful students piloted some of the steps.

Principal Kelly O'Connell at Mars Estates Elementary for promoting the art of book writing.

Stella, who wrote her own wonderful children's book following the steps in the book. Her mother, Neelah, learned the process and photographed her daughter's writing.

About the Author

Pat Goldys was born in Baltimore, Maryland and lived there for 63 years. She loves steamed crabs, carmel creams and snowballs. She moved to Florida to be near her granddaughter, Mila.

Pat continues to write stories about real events, as well as the make believe. Kids like fiction and nonfiction. She writes stories that kids like to read and parents and grandparents can read to their children.

Note to Teacher

This guide is easy for both student and teacher. The lessons can be independently done by students in grades to 2-5 and beyond. The lessons can be shared by teacher or parent.

Here is how!

1. We Do: Read the story in "Get Ready!" Section. Have children pair/share their responses. Children learn what kind of writers they are. Chart responses as a prep for the writing process.

2. Teachers Do: Model each step by reading poem, then do a think aloud of how you would do each step.

3. Students Do: Use the modeling from the teacher and the writing samples provided. Students can practice, explore, and WRITE RIGHT IN THE BOOK!

Dear Aspiring Writer,

You can do this! Everyone has their story. Think about it and write it down. Every story can be your book.

This book will take you on a journey to create your very own book. This book is organized to teach, guide, model and actually write a book!

The first part is a motivational message to encourage you to start the process. Then there is a poem to explain each step. There are specific directions and models to make the process easy to do. Then you get an opportunity to practice what you learned.

Writers have different ways to accomplish their books. There are different ways to understand the process. You can use the poem to stimulate your creativity. You can read the easy-to-follow directions. You can use the models to see exactly what you need to do.

At the end of this book, you will have your own book! You will do each part of the writing process till you get to publishing—— and then this is the book that you wrote!

Read it to everyone!

Get ready! Get set! Write!

YOUR AUTHOR ADVENTURE
BEGINS HERE!

Get ready! Get set! Write!

LET'S GET READY!

I can be an author at any age!
As long as I have a paper and pencil to start
a page.
I think about what I can write.
Then I write and write all through the night.
WHAT DO YOU LIKE ABOUT WRITING?

I can be an author at any time!
Be it morning or the night.
When an idea pops in my head,
I write it down on paper next
to my bed.
WHEN DO YOU LIKE TO WRITE?

I can be an author at any place.

In school, outside, in outer space.

I just write the words that do explain

A story when read that will also entertain.

WHERE DO YOU LIKE TO WRITE?

I can be an author of a story

Short or long as I want it to be.

Be it funny, sad, silly or happy.

I am free to write what you will see.

WHAT KIND OF STORIES DO YOU WRITE?

I can be an author, tell me how!

I will write my story, starting now!

I will be an author writing what I know!

I will be an author, ready, set, go!

WHAT DO YOU NEED TO START YOUR WRITING ADVENTURE?

LET'S GET SET!

How do you write a book?

Everyone does it their own way.

Here are 10 steps in the writing process.

It is not always a straight line. Sometimes you go back and forth in the steps when you write.

Writing a book takes time. Be patient with your creativity.

What will you write about?

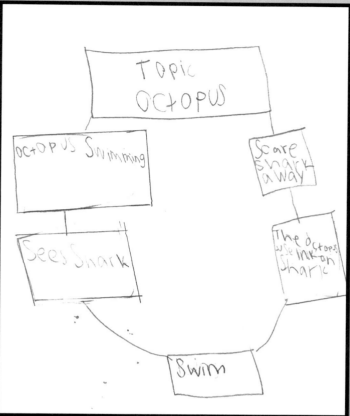

What will you write about?

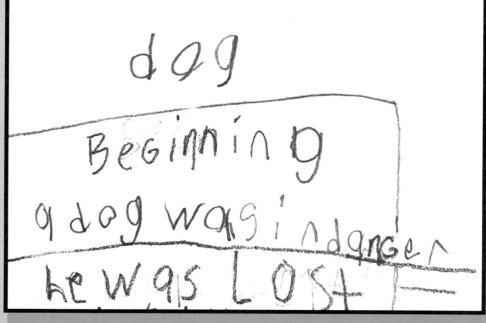

It's messy! Crossing out.
Erasing. Redoing. Be kind to yourself. Be
courageous and reflective and understanding
of all your mistakes. Your mistakes are risks
you take to create a children's book.

This third grade class practiced the writing
steps. These *Drafts* tell them that they can
write and be an author!

Persistence!

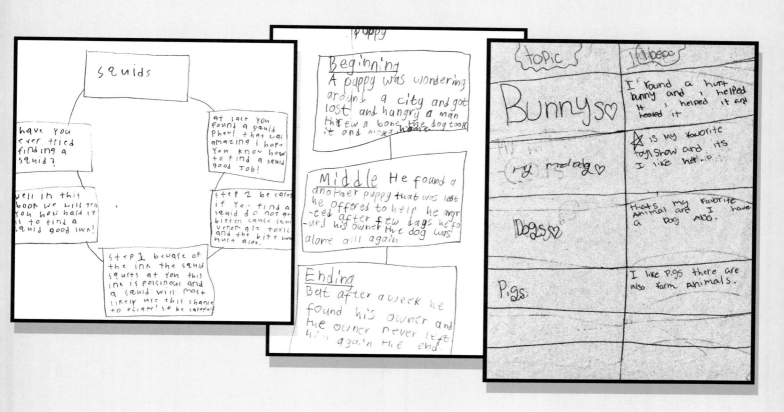

Squids

have you ever tried finding a squid?

well in this book we will tell you how hard it is to find a squid good luck!

at last you found a squid phew! that was amazing i hope you know how to find a squid good job!

step 2 be careful if you find a squid do not get bitten cause squid venom is toxic and the bite will hurt alot.

step 1 beware of the ink the squid squirts at you this ink is poisonous and a squid will most likely use this chance to escape! so be careful

puppy

Beginning
A puppy was wondering around a city and got lost and hangry a man threw a bone the dog took it and made a home.

Middle He found a another puppy that was lost he offered to help he agreed after few days he found his owner the dog was alone all again

Ending
But after a week he found his owner and the owner never left him again the end.

topic — **idea**

Bunnys♡ — I found a hurt bunny and i helped it healed it

My — ry melody♡ — is my favorite toy show and its I like her..p..

Dogs♡ — thats my favorite Animal and I have a dog Also.

Pigs — I like pigs there are also farm Animals.

Perseverance!

One Day i was in My Back yard And then i saw a kitty cat. then i Pick it up And He was Black. His eyes Shine Like the Sun! He was so Adorable. i was About to Leave. then the Next Day He was there! every Day He come i give Him Food And i call Him Luca. we adopt Him ♡

Walking my dog at the Park

I am in the house and geting The leash for my dog now I am out side and I am in the Park and walking her in The Park and then I lost! my dog and I was worried and i was finding her and then I found her.

Doing My Chores

One day it was a saturday the day

I had chores it was that I had to walk my little brother so I did it but after that week there was a problem my brother had Stomoch I quirkly Ran for mediche but it close early So I was worried my last thing I did was that I gave him cold water and after 5 minutes it work So I walked Him.

Courage!

Critical Thinking!

Topic ♡	Idea ♡
bunnies	how to get a bunny
fish	getting a fish
friend	making a friend
dogs	getting a dog
cats	getting a cat

Topic	idea
History	learning about History
meditation	trying to meditate
Pencils	materials for pencils
Love ♡	learning about Love
Kids	being a kid

Creative Thinking

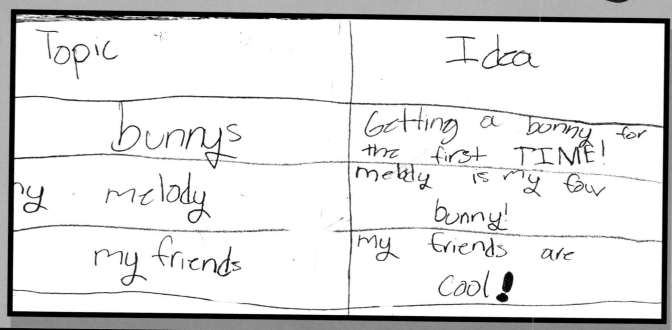

Topic	Idea
bunnys	Getting a bunny for the first TIME!
my melody	melody is my fav bunny!
my friends	my friends are cool!

Beginning the cat went to the forest and a fox came out of no were and stok his food and the cat was sad.

Middle then the cat stok the fox food and the fox was mad he tride to get reveng then he went to find the cat.

Ending then when he found the cat he ran to get reveng and the cat ran inside. the cat was saft inside and the fox ran away becaduse.

I walk my cat and see a LO and I Like whan I see a cat. and I Love them. they are so adorable and so cute and so betfue and so nice when i see a another on and I mean they can be mean some times and be away for me you and cat are not fun to Play with !! when and I LOOK At a cat it LOOK mean and whan I talk to the cat it dont answer.

I was having a nice day and I go to my phone but it was gone. I asked everyon in my family and everyone said no. Then I saw my phone in my brother's hand so I ask for it and He said no. so I told my mom and I got my phone back.

Draft

Tolerance!

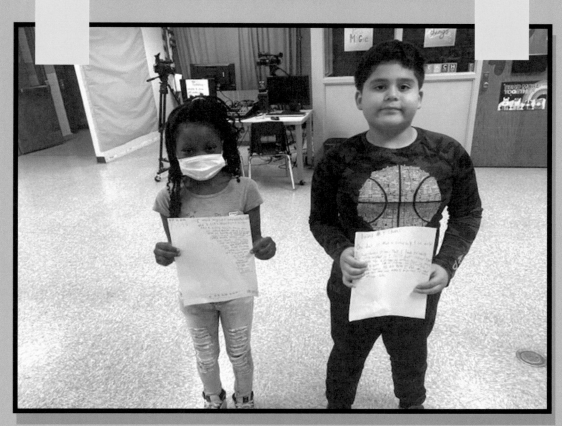

LET'S WRITE!

Brainstorming

I think about a special moment in time.
I think about topics I can refine.
I think about what I know.
Then I take that idea and make it grow.

You do

1. List all your topics, then expand it into an idea that can become a story.

Topic	Idea
dolphin	saving a dolphin
cat	smelly cat no one want
party	different places
Thanksgiving	no turkey goes bad
zoo	animals in differe cages
bike ride	with mag glasses

Topic	Idea

Outlining

Draw a web to organize.

This is how to strategize

Exactly how to sequence the events.

So a story to the reader makes more sense.

You do

1. Make a web and list details about your idea.

2. Decide what ideas are in the beginning, middle and ending.

3. Sequence the details from the web into beginning, middle, ending

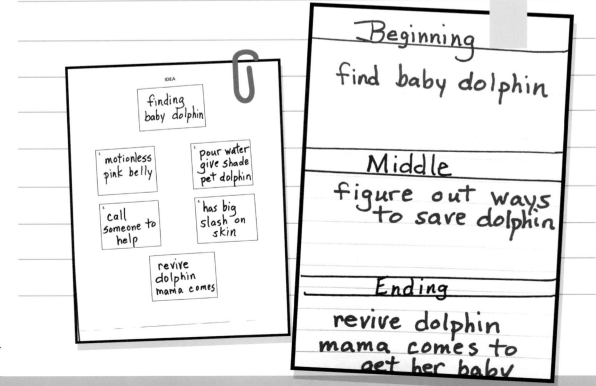

IDEA

finding baby dolphin

1. motionless pink belly

2. pour water give shade pet dolphin

3. call someone to help

4. has big slash on skin

revive dolphin mama comes

Beginning

find baby dolphin

Middle

figure out ways to save dolphin

Ending

revive dolphin mama comes to get her baby

IDEA

BEGINNING

MIDDLE

END

Drafting

I write and write my ideas galore.

Then read my draft, I want to make sure,

It has all the details I need before

I decide I will have to write more.

I take this draft and see it in my head.

The story emerging from the ideas I said.

I read and write and read and write so I can tell,

If everything I captured is written well!

You do

1. Look at your outline and start writing SENTENCES, starting at the beginning. Write out a draft of your story.

2. Don't worry about mistakes. This is a time to free flow with your ideas. When done with the first draft, rehearse(reread) draft to yourself. Make changes you see as necessary.

3. Then rehearse your story with anyone who will listen and give you feedback.

4. Change to make better.

5. Write your sentences.

Note to writer: The letters (ARMS and CUPS) on the draft papers are needed for revisions and editing. You will learn that later in the book.

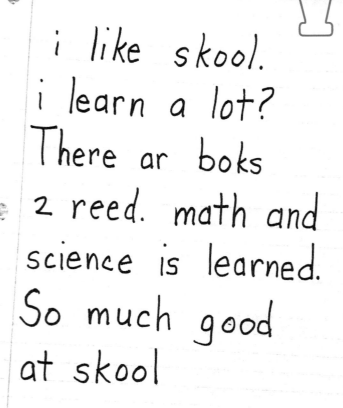

i like skool.
i learn a lot?
There ar boks
2 reed. math and
science is learned.
So much good
at skool

A
R
M
S

C
U
P
S

Feedback

Rehearse your story over and over making reflections.

Have lots of readers give thoughtful suggestions.

Think about the praise, questions and improvements to make.

This feedback is needed to help fix mistakes.

You do

1. Have someone listen to you read your story.

2. Give them a form to write:

*what they like

*ask for clarification

*parts for improvement

*any other thoughts they have on what you wrote.

3. Reflect on their feedback and make changes as you decide are needed.

4. Others' feedback are a GIFT to you. It makes your book better.

> Good: Complete sentences with descriptive words.
>
> Inquire: What make school fun?
>
> Fix: Add adverbs to visualize the actions.
>
> Thoughts: Rehearse it.

good

Inquire?

Fix

Thoughts

Revise

I like to revise my ideas to make things clear.
Ask me questions, give suggestions that are
sincere.
Revision is a time for changes to expand
And make the story easy to understand.

You do

1. Select a peer reviser. It can be a teacher,
parent, grandparent, fellow student, or friend.
2. Show them how to revise below. Have reviser
use the revision checklist on the draft.

A Add on to clarify.
R Remove if not adding to story.
M Move to different part of story.
S Substitute a better word or sentence to
add power to story.

3. Reflect on all your revisions on the checklist
and make changes you agree with.
4. At this time, reread and create a title for
your book.

i like skool.
i ~~learn~~ think (s) a lot?
There ar boks
2 reed. ~~Do you~~ (R)
~~like candy~~? What
happens at school? math
and science is learned
So much good (A) ^and fun^ at
skool

Did you or a friend...

Add +

Remove -

Move

Substitute

Editing

After revision, I edit a lot.

Finding capitals, punctuation and spelling spots,

That need some fixing so all can read.

Making sure it is good before I proceed.

I take a rubric or checklist with editing rules.

I must be patient and proofread, an important

writing tool.

You do

1. Select a peer editor. It can be a teacher, parent, grandparent, fellow student, or friend.

I like school.

I learn a lot?

There are books.

to read. Do you like candy? Math and science are learned. So much good at school!

2. Show them how to edit below.

C **Capitalization**
U **Usage**
P **Punctuation**
S **Spelling**

3. Reflect on all your edits and make changes you agree with.

4. You can either put the letter on top of what needs to change OR you can cross out and make change.

Did you or a friend...

Check capitals

Check usage

Check punctuation

Check spelling

Practice revising and editing.

Doing My Chores

One day it Was a Saturday, the day I had chores. It was that I had to walk my little brother. So I did it but after that week there was a problem. My brother had a stomachache. I quickly ran for medicine but closed early. So I was worried. My last thing I did was that I gave him cold Water and after 5 minutes it worked. So I walked him. I finished (Add) the store (s) all my chores

One day I have a pet hamster Rose I was play with her one day she got lost and I need to find one day I made food for the hamster when I wait she come. I wait and wait but head something I look and se she come back an that food. Might made her hungry.

This cat is my cat and her name is mimi. and she loves to go outside. but one Day she ran away i went looking for her and we found mimi!!

Walking my dog at the Park

I am in the house and getting the leash for my dog now I am out side and I am in the park and walking her in the park and then I lost! my dog and I was worried and i was finding her and then I found her.

Rewriting

My friend helped me edit and revise

In case I missed something and needed some advice.

It's still not done, I fix over and over again.

I keep adding, moving, changing, and then

After rereading and rewriting, it can

Be published for every girl and boy

To read as they laugh, smile and share with joy.

You do

1. Place page with revisions and editing side by side as you copy the corrected sentences.

2. This is a tedious task, but must be done. Your published book must be error free if read by others.

3. Reread and correct anything that still needs to be revised or edited.

4. Rewrite text and do cover on following pages.

Illustrating

Read your text to clarify.

Visualize in your head and identify

What you will draw to show

Exactly what to see and know

In the story you did write

To know what is happening at first sight.

You do

1. Reread your pages.

2. Draw exactly what the text says.

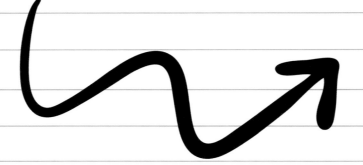

3. After drawing, reread and make sure the illustration matches the text.

The Beach

We go to the beach. We build sand castles. We collect shells. A crab hid in the sand. There's so many fish in our bucket! So much sun and fun!

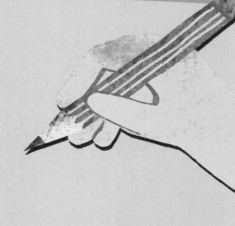

Draw your cover

Summary

Additional Features

Dedication page is who you wrote the book for,
Someone that helped you, that you adore!

Dedication:
To all the animals that live in the parks, the people who visit
the parks, and the park rangers who are dedicated to the care
of the parks!

Biography is all about you.
Write about what you wish people knew
About the author of this book.
Give the reader an inside look!

Pat Goldys was born in Baltimore, Maryland and
lived there for 63 years. She loves steamed
crabs, carmel creams and snowballs. She moved
to Florida to be near her granddaughter, Mila.
Pat continues to write stories about real
events, as well as the make believe. She writes
stories that kids like to read and parents and
grandparents can read to their children.

Summary is on the back cover.

A paragraph about what one will discover when they read the story inside that the author wrote with great pride!

   When Adam and Grandma do shopping, they come home with more than just groceries. Ernie, the deaf dog, was lost and had no where to go. Grandma and Adam find him and decide to keep him. Ernie learns the signs that Adam teaches him and becomes Ernie the lucky, and very much loved dog.

You do

1. Dedication—When you write a book, you are creating something magical and amazing. There are people who helped you or you thought of while writing it. It is an honor to dedicate a book to someone you adore!

2. Biography—Everybody wants to know a little something about the author. Write some details about who you are and about what you like.

3. Summary—Write a few sentences to get a reader excited to read your book!

Dedication:

Biography:

Summary:

Publishing and Celebrating

I am so excited my story has been told.

I want you to read it if I can be so bold.

I want to celebrate so you can hear

My words of action and description, strong and clear!

I can read my book at many different places!

In front of many listening faces

To animals at the farm or zoo

Before bed, in the library too

On a tractor or a truck or bus

To another class and video us!

I wrote my own book!

And everyone needs to take a look!

Different Ways to Celebrate!

1. Read book to another class.
2. Have an Author's Tea and read to parents.
3. Tape the reading of your book.
4. Read your book to a group at the county or school library.
5. Send a copy of your book to your grandparents.

CONGRATULATIONS TO YOU!
You are an author!

I did it! I wrote this book!

Stella wrote an amazing book! She followed the process! It took her 3.5 hours to make her book. She said there was a party going on in her head!

TOPIC	IDEA
Cats	Has A worry
Farm	lives In A Barn
Animals	Feathers and Birds
Gems	See's A Gem Path

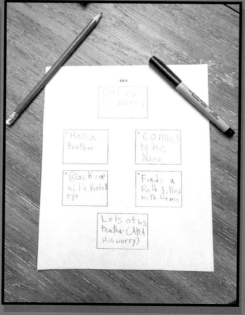

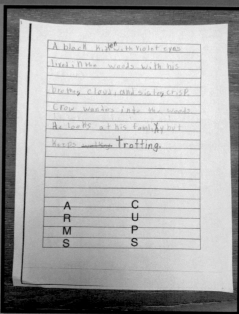

Kit lives in the woods with his brothers and sisters. Finds a Feather keeps it with him.

MIDDLE

(skip to 2 months latter) Cat walks through to the barn but sees a gem Path and dosn't Know why he's scared.

ENDING

Sleeping, wind took it and he wakes up and Runs off after it and caught it but somthing hits him and he Relises he should let it go and runs into the sunflower Patch and lets it go. A Bear, heron all of its gonna land on one...

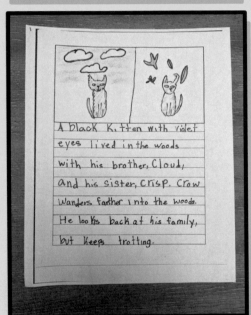

A black Kitten with violet eyes lived in the woods with his brother, Cloud, and his sister, Crisp. Crow Wanders farther into the woods. He looks back at his family, but keeps trotting.

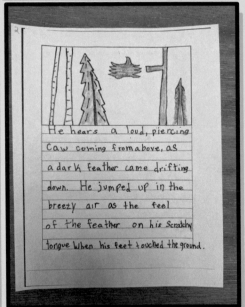

He hears a loud, piercing Caw coming from above, as a dark feather came drifting down. He jumped up in the breezy air as the feel of the feather on his scratchy tongue when his feet touched the ground.

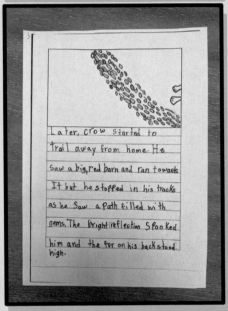

Later, crow started to trail away from home. He saw a big, red barn and ran towards it but he stopped in his tracks as he saw a path filled with gems. The bright reflection spooked him and the fur on his back stood high.

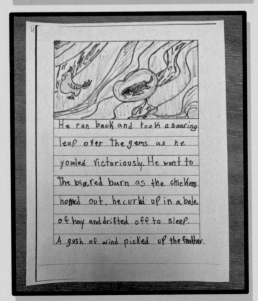

He ran back and took a soaring leap over the gems as he yowled victoriously. He went to the big, red barn as the chickens hopped out, he curled up in a bale of hay and drifted off to sleep. A gush of wind picked up the feather.

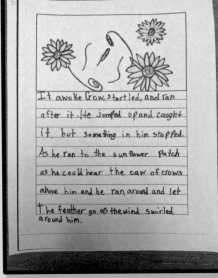

It awoke Crow, startled, and ran after it. He jumped up and caught it, but something in him stopped. As he ran to the sunflower Patch as he could hear the caw of crows above him and he ran around and let the feather go as the wind swirled around him.

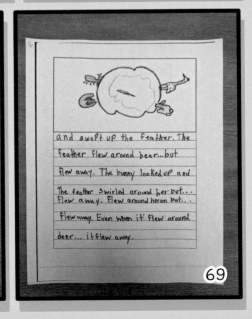

and swept up the feather. The feather flew around bear...but flew away. The bunny looked up and the feather swirled around her but... flew away. Flew around heron but... flew away. Even when it flew around deer... it flew away.

69

Book Summary

This book is about
- letting go
- facing your fears
- and family.

Dedicated to:

Chris Tudor, owner of the farm!
Stella's favorite place

Note From Author — "Remember to always let go of your worries!"

Biography

Stella likes chickens and helping out at the farm. She is a loving sister and daughter and kind to all she meets.

Author Discussion

1. Which part was the hardest? Why?

2. Which part was the most fun? Why?

3. What do you want to improve? Why?

4. What is the next book you will write? Why?

This is not **THE END**.

This is **THE BEGINNING**
of your adventures as an author.
Keep writing!

Glossary

Brainstorm—— develop creative ideas and list them

Edit—— correct the mechanics of your writing. Change the capitals, look for correct sentence structure and neatness, review for periods, question marks and exclamation marks, and check if words are spelled correctly

Draft—— free-writing and free flow of ideas that will become your story. Don't worry about mistakes. You can edit and revise later

Feedback—— provide the author with suggestions to make the writing better. Share what is good, ask about what you don't understand, and share your thoughts about editing and revising that you see necessary

Outline—— organize the events that are in the beginning, middle and ending of story

Publish—— get your story in book form and share with others in any way that people can hear or read the book

Rehearse—— reread your story over and over again to yourself and others

Revise—— review the content of your story. Add words/sentences to make it better, move sentences, remove sentences that don't belong, substitute one word for a better word

Rewrite—— take your edited and revised sentences and make the corrections so it can be read by others